Forty Penances
for Spiritual Exercise

living the great gift of mercy

Stephen Joseph Wolf

Forty Penances for Spiritual Exercise
Copyright © 2014
Stephen Joseph Wolf
All rights reserved.
No part of this book may be copied or reproduced
in any form or by any means without the written
permission of the publisher, except for the inclusion
of brief quotations in a review.

Scripture texts in this work are taken from the
New American Bible, revised edition, © 2010, 1991, 1986, 1970
Confraternity of Christian Doctrine, Inc., Washington, DC.
All Rights Reserved.

Songs are in the public domain and previously appeared in
Hinge Hour Singer, idjc press, 2011.

Stephen Joseph Wolf is a parish priest in Nashville
who spends most Mondays in silence and solitude
writing for faith-sharing groups and spiritual direction.

idjc press books
are distributed by Ingram Books;
for more visit **www.idjc.org.**

ISBN 978-1-937081-06-5

other six-chapter titles for faith-sharing groups:

Tree of Life, Saint Bonaventure on the Christ Story
Pondering Our Faith, Revised with the New Creed
Twelve-Step Spirituality for Christians
God's Money
Anger-Grief the Jesus Way
Planning My Own Funeral? (4 weeks)

idjc.org

dedicated to parish priests
celebrating week after week
the sacrament of reconciliation

How to use these *Forty Penances*

These exercises have two kinds of users in mind.

1st - an Individual Seeker

reflecting on how the Lord is moving in your life:

> Take the time to go slowly, and keep it simple.
>
> Wherever you find yourself drawn,
> linger for pondering, perhaps breathing
> with a particular word or phrase.
>
> Consider one exercise each day for forty days.

2nd – a Faith Sharing Group

perhaps meeting over six weeks:

> Use what is helpful and ignore the rest;
> keep it simple.
>
> If someone in the group knows the song,
> you have a song leader. If one person leads
> the rest can follow; the tunes are simple
> and from the Church tradition.
>
> Group members can take turns being the *Leader*
> week to week, but it works best if there is only
> one *Leader* of each session.
>
> Within each session, group members can take
> turns being the *Reader*, though no one should
> be compelled to be a *Reader*.
>
> The *Leader* is encouraged to allow, by timing it,
> one full minute of silence before announcing
> the next exercise.

But keep it simple.

FORTY PENANCES for Spiritual Exercise
living the great gift of mercy

Introduction   7

1st Week
Reality of God's Complete Love   11
  1 Psalm 46
  2 Psalm 131
  3 A Tree Gives Glory to God By…
  4 Isaiah 43:1-5
  5 A Walk to Search for Beauty
  6 Psalm 104
  7 God's Ones

2nd Week
Reality of Sin and Reconciliation   29
  8 The Lord's Prayer and/or Psalm 23
  9 Un-telling a Lie
 10 Remembering your Baptism
 11 One Freely Done Tithe
 12 The Prologue of John
 13 Immensity and Absurdity of Sin
 14 Who Am I That You Care For Me?

3rd Week
Universal Call to Holiness   43
 15 Psalm 65
 16 Love is Patient; Love is Kind…
 17 *Lectio Divina* at Mass
 18 72 Tools of the Spiritual Craft
 19 Naming My Cross

- 20 What's Missing?
- 21 My Favorite Gospel Story

4th Week

Vocation "Yes"   61
- 22 I Have Called You Friends
- 23 Anger the Jesus Way
- 24 Ask To See What God Sees
- 25 Saint Benedict's Twelve Steps to Humility
- 26 The Song that Makes Me Say "YES!"
- 27 Calendar, Closet, Checkbook and Will
- 28 The At-Hand Stretch

5th Week

Perfect Act of Love   77
- 29 God's Truth, or Psalm 27
- 30 Letter to the Romans, or Romans 8
- 31 The Greatest Command
- 32 Flip Through the Book of Psalms
- 33 A Busy Day for Jesus
- 34 To Bed One Hour Early
- 35 The 2nd Letter of John

6th Week

Wholly New Way   91
- 36 Four (or Five) toward Intimacy
- 37 One of the Last Five Psalms
- 38 First Chapter of a Gospel
- 39 The Breath of the Risen Lord
- 40 Claiming Apostleship

Going to Confession   105
Acknowledgments   108

Introduction

I think in rows and columns. Can't help it. Having worked as an accountant for fourteen tax seasons, something happened in my brain and I think in columns and rows. A couple of years ago while praying about it being time again to go to confession myself, a scribbled list of penances came forth, forty of them, forty penances for which people had later returned with gratitude.

Pondering them, I saw a spreadsheet of parish spirituality, intersections of Trappist with Jesuit and Franciscan with the Rule of Saint Benedict. Giving them a rough order along the lines of the *Spiritual Exercises* laid out by Saint Ignatius of Loyola seemed a natural thing to do.

This may have been nothing more than a distraction from my own need for the sacrament of reconciliation. Still, I used this outline on some retreats and it seemed helpful. So, here it is.

Some Catholics have forgotten that part of the sacrament of Reconciliation-Confession-Penance is *accepting* the penance suggested by the priest. You can ask for a different penance.

Since the point of a penance is not to *earn* forgiveness but to *celebrate* it, I have tried to avoid naming the sin that might prompt a penance. There might not be just one!

So what is a sin?* To be a *sin* the thing has to cross three thresholds. The priest is listening for an action (or an omission) that is

> 1st wrong, ***and***
> 2nd known by the person to be wrong, ***and***
> 3rd freely done (or freely omitted).

Just so you know. (See also paragraphs 1846-76 of the Catechism.)

Take a look at those three. Indeed, there are times when someone is very sorry for something that is not really a sin, because it is simply not wrong. You and I may see someone doing something that looks just plain wrong, but it may not be a sin because the person doing it does not know it is wrong. And there is a lot of bad doing that is not a sin because it is done by a person who is not acting in freedom.

This underscores the vocation of the serious and good work of conscience formation.

This is also why the job of judging is God's job alone. The rest of us do not have enough data. We may be capable to judge that something is wrong, but you and I can never judge whether someone else has sinned.

These forty penances all surfaced in the midst of celebrations of the sacrament. I have learned to simply trust the better-than-even chance that they come from the Holy Spirit and go from there.

Reconciliation is more about God's mercy than anything else.

Early in the Gospel of Mark (2:1-12) a paralyzed man is brought to Jesus by his friends. Jesus is so impressed with the faith of the friends and their love for this soul that he gives him the greatest of God's many gifts: mercy.

The *powers that be* did not like this uppity action because, as they said, only God can forgive sins. Jesus sees again the greatest gift from God being ridiculed by the *powers that be*. So as a kind of proof, that they might know that the Son of Man has *authority* to forgive sins, he tells the paralyzed man, "Rise, pick up your mat, and go."

We ask God for all kinds of things, and that is great as far as it goes. This healing story reminds me that God has indeed created a world with an abundance for all, and the bulk of the human suffering which does not have to happen does happen because of human selfishness. The real gift of the Giver is loving-mercy, merciful-love, the mercy that requires power and authority.

My hope is that even one of these spiritual exercises might help you to celebrate this great gift of God's mercy.

Rev. Steve Wolf

Songs of thankfulness and praise,
Jesus, Lord, to you we raise,
Manifested by the star
To the magi from afar;
Branch of roy/-al David's stem
In your birth at Bethlehem;
Praises be to you addressed,
God in flesh made manifest.

Manifest at Jordan's stream,
Prophet, Priest and King supreme;
And as Cana's wedding guest,
In your Godhead manifest;
Manifest/ in pow'r divine,
Changing water into wine;
Praises be to you addressed,
God in flesh made manifest.

Grant us grace to see you, Lord,
Mirrored in your holy Word;
May our imitation show,
In your likeness may we grow;
Pure and ho/-ly may we be
At your great Epiphany;
May we praise you, ever blest,
God in flesh made manifest.

> Text: Christopher Wordsworth, 1862, altered
> Music: 77 77 D, SALZBURG; Jakob Hintze, 1678

Exercises 1-7
(1st Week)
Reality of God's Complete Love

SONG (from page 10), all together

LEADER:

Listen to a love letter from God to you:

> My Beloved,
> I have made you in my image, one and unique,
> not like anyone ever has been
> or ever will be made in my image.
> Having made you, I know you, all the
> great things your ego wants everyone to know,
> those things you do not want anyone to know,
> and everything you do not yet know yourself.
> And in knowing you, I love you,
> neither because of your strengths
> nor in spite of your weaknesses;
> there is nothing you can do
> that will make me love you,
> and there is nothing you can do
> that will keep me from loving you.
> Remember this always: that I love you just is.
> — God

Pause for one minute of silence now and after each exercise.

1

Psalm 46

Stress can be called a "condition for the possibility" or a "near occasion" for many kinds of sin. A sin is often a very human response to stress. Suitable for many a penance, Psalm 46 gives a picture of stressful trouble: earthquake, storm, mountains falling into the sea… Note the words God uses to cut through it.

One good way to pray with most psalms is called *lectio divina* ('lek-see-oh div-'ee-nuh), which begins with listening for, even choosing, the word or phrase that speaks to you, and sitting for a bit to breathe and repeat the word or phrase until you exhaust it, or it exhausts you.

One monk's take: *Sit with it without thinking about it*. Many like to sit with what a friend called *the phrase that prays* for 20 minutes to an hour, but a penance has to be do-able. So the usual suggestion is for a few minutes.

Whenever a penance is a scripture passage, "if you forget which scripture to pray, let the Lord lead you to a better one."

Psalm 46

God is our refuge and our strength,
an ever-present help in distress.
Thus we do not fear, though earth be shaken
and mountains quake to the depths of the sea,
Though its waters rage and foam
and mountains totter at its surging.

Streams of the river gladden the city of God,
the holy dwelling of the Most High.
God is in its midst; it shall not be shaken;
God will help it at break of day.
Though nations rage and kingdoms totter,
he utters his voice and the earth melts.
The Lord of hosts is with us;
our stronghold is the God of Jacob.

Come and see the works of the Lord,
who has done fearsome deeds on earth;
Who stops wars to the ends of the earth,
breaks the bow, splinters the spear,
and burns the shields with fire;
"Be still and know that I am God!
  I am exalted among the nations,
  exalted on the earth."
The Lord of hosts is with us;
our stronghold is the God of Jacob.

2

Psalm 131

God is God and I am not. God is God and my parents are not. And yet, God has used my parents, even in their imperfection and humanity, to say to me *something* (not everything but *something*) about who God is.

My suspicion is that the 4th commandment, to honor our parents, is rooted more in this mystery than in either the concepts of justice and mercy or the best ethic of society providing for the elderly, as wise as those teachings are.

Psalm 131

> Lord, my heart is not proud;
> nor are my eyes haughty.
> I do not busy myself with great matters,
> with things too sublime for me.
> Rather, I have stilled my soul,
> Like a weaned child to its mother,
> weaned is my soul.
> Israel, hope in the Lord,
> now and forever.

3

A Tree Gives Glory To God By...

Does cheating come from belief in the big lie that "I am not good enough"? Each of us is made in God's image in a unique way. No one ever has been or ever will be made in God's image in this particular way. God does not ask any of us to become someone else; rather God is asking each of us to let God keep forming and growing us into that one human person God created us to be.

Take a walk and look for a tree that grabs you. If you cannot walk or go outside, call to mind a tree in your imagination or from your memory. Get close enough, and far enough away, to let the tree fill up your whole frame of vision: the tree is all you see. Breathe, and repeat these words in your heart:

A tree gives glory to God by being a tree.

Thomas Merton (Trappist Monk)
New Seeds of Contemplation
© 1961 Abbey of Gethsemani, Inc.

Consider inserting your name:

_____ gives glory to God by being _____.

4

Isaiah 43:1-5

Is it possible for God to work through a good counselor? You bet. In my first adult encounter with depression, healing happened in a religious experience. Part of the groundwork for that conversion was a simple and profound exercise suggested by my counselor. Linda asked me to make a list of my strengths and weaknesses. It may help here to know I was a certified public accountant before entering seminary. Now having been a priest longer than I was an accountant, still I think in columns and rows.

After a few days of pondering, finishing one tax return before starting on the next, I scratched out a list. There were more weaknesses than strengths. Gazing on the sacred scratch pad, debits and credits began to line up. Surprise! For each of the few strengths there was a weakness to match it. Then I was able to name offsetting strengths for the rest of the weaknesses. The debits and the credits were in balance. At least I thought they were.

The next counseling session, eager was I to go over my new balance sheet. Linda simply smiled and instead asked me to fold the weaknesses behind the strengths, and several times a day to look at only the strengths. It was a task almost impossible. My suspicion has since been that after three decades of trying to eradicate my shortcomings, they had become the lens through which I saw myself. The big surprise was how painful it was to keep admitting that I have gifts. Often do I recognize this in people around me. So here is one retired accountant's take on the balance sheet of a human person created in the image of God:

BAPTIZED* HUMAN PERSON
BALANCE SHEET
FROM CONCEPTION TO DEATH

ASSETS	LIABILITIES & NET WORTH
Unique Creation	~~Original Sin~~*
Natural Talents	Human Weakness
Human Virtues	Sinful Tendencies
Faith/Hope/Love	TOTAL LIABILITIES
Charisms	*Imago Dei***
TOTAL ASSETS =	TOTAL LIABILITIES & NET WORTH

** In accounting this part of the balance sheet is called "equity," or "net worth."

In the human person, created in the image of God, the value, weight, significance, goodness, etc. (*assets?*) will **always** be greater than that of the weaknesses (*liabilities?*) of that person. In double entry accounting, this difference is called "net worth." Can we call this excess the stamp of the image of God, the *imago dei*? This can never be taken away. And there is more.

God does not love us only because of our goodness, and God will not stop loving us because of our weakness, or even sin. There is nothing that we can do to make God love us, and there is nothing that we can do that will keep God from loving us. That God loves us simply is. How many of us spend our entire lives coming to terms with this truth!

So, what is the penance? It is the most difficult passage that I have ever prayed, and I do not suggest it at random. I will find myself telling the penitent that there is a penance that is only for those who can handle it; "do you think you can handle it?" No one has yet asked for a lighter one.

Ask God whether God wants you to hear these words. Insert your name into this love letter delivered for all time through the prophet Isaiah, and let your God speak it to you:

Isaiah 43:1-5a

But now, thus says the Lord,
who created you, _____,
and formed you, _____:
Do not fear,
for I have redeemed you;
I have called you by name:
you are mine.
When you pass through waters,
I will be with you;
through rivers,
you shall not be swept away.
When you walk through fire,
you shall not be burned,
nor will flames consume you.
For I, the Lord, am your God,
the Holy One of _____, your savior.
I give…ransom for you…
Because you are precious in my eyes
and honored,
and I love you,
I give (a ransom)
…in exchange for your life.
Fear not, for I am with you…

5

A Walk to Search for Beauty

Can you name something like money or porn or prestige that you are treating as an idol?

Take a walk. If you want your walk to be in nature's beauty, fine. You can do this one on the street where you live or where you work. Just take a walk, and look for things beautiful.

When you sense something beautiful, a cloud or bird or garden or architecture or tree or children playing or car or squirrel or clean house or radio music or jogger or kite flying or paint job or good natured arguing or driver singing or well cut lawn or well dressed neighbor or dog or cat or creek or flower or or or... When you sense it stop!

Acknowledge in your heart the beauty you see! And thank God, who is so far beyond the human categories for beauty that saints have called God *Beauty-Itself*. Thank God also for the gifts of being able to notice and give thanks.

While walking and noticing and thanking, remember to breathe.

6
Psalm 104

When life goes from hum to drum its meaning can get lost in boredom. *There are no boring days; only boring people:* words spoken by a college friend and I wanted to hit him. My real fear was that I might be a boring person. How much acting out do we do in the pride-filled reach for relevant recognition?

A Benedictine monk at the Saint Meinrad monastery shares a helpful mantra:

Humility is reality; pride is illusion.

In a full day of hiking and breathing these words, I added a third piece:

Humility is reality;
pride is illusion;
fear too: illusion.

We make our journey as pilgrims and not as wandering nomads. We have a destination (heaven) while also called to help build up the kingdom of God here and now. When one's gifts aren't used, a pilgrim can be easily bored.

And what does boredom have to do with pride? If I take myself too seriously, if I think I am too good for this world/family/business/community, if the world is not doing a very good job of entertaining me, then my view of myself is way yonder beyond too serious.

An antidote for this state of being can be to step back and take a good gander at all of creation and by God's grace see our place in it that is so significant without having to always seem to be. Take a breath for a longer psalm:

Psalm 104

> Bless the Lord, my soul!
> Lord, my God, you are great indeed!
> You are clothed with majesty and splendor,
> robed in light as with a cloak.
> You spread out the heavens like a tent;
> setting the beams of your chambers
> upon the waters.
> You make the clouds your chariot;
> traveling on the wings of the wind.
> You make the winds your messengers;
> flaming fire, your ministers.

You fixed the earth on its foundation,
so it can never be shaken.
The deeps covered it like a garment;
above the mountains stood the waters.
At your rebuke they took flight;
at the sound of your thunder they fled.
They rushed up the mountains,
down the valleys
to the place you had fixed for them.
You set a limit they cannot pass;
never again will they cover the earth.

You made springs flow in wadies
that wind among the mountains.
They give drink to every beast of the field;
here wild asses quench their thirst.
Beside them the birds of heaven nest;
among the branches they sing.
You water the mountains from your chambers;
from the fruit of your labor the earth abounds.
You make the grass grow for the cattle
and plants for people's work
to bring forth food from the earth,
wine to gladden their hearts,
oil to make their faces shine,
and bread to sustain the human heart.

The trees of the Lord drink their fill,
the cedars of Lebanon, which you planted.
There the birds build their nests;
the stork in the junipers, its home.
The high mountains are for wild goats;
the rocky cliffs, a refuge for badgers.

You made the moon to mark the seasons,
the sun that knows the hour of its setting.
You bring darkness and night falls,
then all the animals of the forest wander about.
Young lions roar for prey;
they seek their food from God.
When the sun rises, they steal away
and settle down in their dens.
People go out to their work,
to their labor till evening falls.

How varied are your works, Lord!
In wisdom you have made them all;
the earth is full of your creatures.
There is the sea, great and wide!
It teems with countless beings,
living things both large and small.
There ships ply their course
and Leviathan, whom you formed to play with.

All of these look to you
to give them food in due time.
When you give it to them, they gather;
when you open your hand, they are well filled.
When you hide your face, they panic.
Take away their breath, they perish
and return to the dust.
Send forth your spirit, they are created
and you renew the face of the earth.

May the glory of the Lord endure forever;
may the Lord be glad in his works!
Who looks at the earth and it trembles,
touches the mountains and they smoke!
I will sing to the Lord all my life;
I will sing praise to my God while I live.
May my meditation be pleasing to him;
I will rejoice in the Lord.
May sinners vanish from the earth,
and the wicked be no more.
Bless the Lord, my soul! Hallelujah!

> *Humility is reality;*
> *pride is illusion;*
> *fear too: illusion.*

A country music song waiting to be written?

7

God's Ones

When Caesar wanted to know how many people were subject to him, he ordered a census, a counting up. When the religious leaders tried to trap Jesus, he asked whose image was stamped on the coin. When they answered, "Caesar's," he said "give to Caesar what is Caesar's and give to God what is God's" (Mark 12:17; Matt 22:21; Luke 20:25).

We human creatures can be counted up, and we encounter limitations of resources. But there is no limit to God's love. And God's complete love for another, even my enemy, takes nothing away from God's complete love for me. Do you believe this? What a world if everyone did.

One of my seminary teachers often used this illustration, of God counting us up, not 1, 2, 3,… …to the 7 billion, but God counts us this way: 1, 1, 1, 1, 1, 1, 1, 1, 1, 1, 1, 1, 1, 1, 1, 1, 1, 1, 1, 1, 1, … each uniquely made in God's image.

The penance: Imagine God taking a census, and when God's finger comes to you, let God's finger rest on your breast, and breathe in God's timeless and infinite love.

Pondering the 1st Week - Exercises 1-7

Ponder in silence whether in Exercises 1 thru 6 something like one of these surfaced:

a seed planted,
something I anticipate taking root and growing within me, and growing me.

a memory provoked,
part of my story, my journey, my identity, whether pleasant or sad.

a question raised,
something unknown suggesting research, discussion with others, or more pondering.

an action prompted or resolution made,
a way God is calling me to become myself.

*Allow at least three minutes for silent pondering,
and then the group may either discuss the ponderings
(restraining the urge to "fix" anybody)
or stay in silence until time is up.*

When time is up: Are there any intercessions from the group?

Our Father ... *and a stanza from the song on page 10?*

There's a wide/-ness in God's mer\-cy
Like the wide-ness of\ the sea;
There's a kind/-ness in God's jus\-tice
Which is more than lib\-er-ty.
There is plen\-ti-ful re-demp\-tion
In the blood/ that has\ been shed;
There\ is joy\ for all\ the mem//\-bers
In the sor\-rows of the Head.

For the love/ of God is broad\-er
Than the meas-ures of\ our mind,
And the heart/ of the E-ter\-nal
Is most won-der-ful\ and kind.
If our love\ were but more simp\-le
We might take/ him at\ his word,
And\ our lives\ would be\ thanks-giv//\-ing
For the good\-ness of the Lord.

Troub-led souls/, why will you scat\-ter
Like a crowd of fright\-ened sheep?
Fool-ish hearts/, why will you wan\-der
From a love so true\ and deep?
There is wel\-come for the sin\-ner
And more gra/-ces for\ the good;
There\ is mer\-cy with\ the Sa//\-vior,
There is heal\-ing in his food.

Text: Frederick W. Fabor, 1814, 1863, altered
Music: 87 87 D, HYFRYDOL; Rowland Prichard, 1811-1887
Popular melody for: *Love Divine, All Love Excelling*

Exercises 8-14
(2nd Week)
Reality of Sin and Reconciliation

SONG (from page 28)

LEADER:

Now and then we meet a person who remains convinced that he or she is not a sinner. I rehearsed the teenage defense I gave my mother: *Look, I haven't killed anybody lately.* When told by a friend, whose mother had already gone to heaven, that when she died I would remember the look on her face, I knew he was right. He was.

One way of seeing *original sin* is as the shared memory in our *dna* or our collective unconscious that reminds us that pushed to a limit we are capable of anything. The sin of Adam and Eve involves a choice you and I would make, and have. Our hope rests in grace telling us we are capable of more.

Sure, those of us who have been baptized are cleansed of *original sin*. But we live with its effects. Like a virus in the air; we still breathe it.

…there is no distinction; all have sinned…

Letter of St. Paul to the Romans 3:22b,23a

Pause for one minute of silence now and after each exercise.

8

The Lord's Prayer and/or Psalm 23

This is one of my favorite penances. It is also a great way to pray with someone who is far away because of travel, work or school.

Imagine that you are sitting with your family or friends, or even with just one person for whom you have concern or feel a need for reconciliation.

Imagine you are sitting in a place familiar to you and to her/him/them. And imagine that Jesus is sitting there too: robes, the beard, the whole get-up. Now pray one *Our Father*, the Lord's Prayer once, one time for both you and your friend or family member(s).

There is a reason we do not call the Lord's Prayer the *"My Father."* Even when I am in my room by myself, to pray ***"Our** Father"* is to pray with the entire universal Church.

Another way to pray this penance is to pray Psalm 23 (*The Lord is my shepherd*) in the form of the "Our Father" (*The Lord is **our** shepherd...*). It is perfectly fine to let Mary and Joseph into the room too.

Psalm 23
In the form of the Our Father

The Lord is *our* shepherd;
there is nothing *we* lack.
In green pastures *our* Lord makes *us* lie down;
to still waters he leads *us*;
he restores *our* soul.

He guides *us* along right paths
for the sake of his name.
Even though *we* walk through the
valley of the shadow of death,
we will fear no evil, for you are with *us*;
your rod and your staff comfort *us*.

You set a table before *us*
in front of our enemies;
you anoint *our* heads with oil;
our cup overflows.

Indeed goodness and mercy will pursue *us*
all the days of *our* lives;
we will dwell in the house of the Lord
for endless days.

9

Un-telling a Lie

The Penance: Call to mind a recent lie you told. Remember walking away from the incident, and in a merging of imagination and memory, ask for the grace of courage and strength to have gone back to the person to whom you lied, saying something like:

> *Got a minute?*
> *That thing I just told you was not true.*
> *I don't know why I said that;*
> *maybe I want you to think well of me,*
> *I don't really know why.*
> *Anyway, this is the truth:_____*
> *Sorry about that. I'll try to not do that again.*
> *Thanks, and sorry again.*

Imagine too a future grace: that the next time you tell a lie, as you walk away from the incident, you ask for the grace of the courage and strength to do this exercise in real life. You won't have to do it very often.

10

Remembering your Baptism

When I do an examination of conscience at the end of a day and am able to name something as sin, which is every day, it seems always to be true that in that particular moment I was not in a state of remembering that God loves me. And it seems rare that I sin while in that remembrance. So here's a mystery for me: Why? Why do I seem unable to remember constantly God's complete love for me and for you? Is this why we return over and over to do Eucharist?

The penance is to go back to the beginning of your Christian life. Most Catholics are baptized as infants, so brain-cell-recall memory is unlikely. Indeed we remember our baptism every Sunday when we profess our faith in the Creed. But this exercise is something a little different.

If you were old enough on the day you were baptized to remember it, this exercise may be easier for you. Simply call up that memory and live it again as described on the next page.

If baptized as an infant, use what you do know about that day and imagine yourself there at the water. There is a priest, deacon, or other baptizer who has gotten you wet and said the words:

_____, *I baptize you in the name of the Father, and of the Son, and of the Holy Spirit.*

You are being held by someone who loves you. Your family and godparents and others who love you are there.

Now remember the story of Jesus' baptism. He rises out of the water. The Spirit descends in the form of a dove. The skies open and a voice declares (in Mark and in Luke), *You are my beloved Son; with you I am well pleased!*

These are words I believe God has been saying to each of us from the day of our birth and baptism. The penance is to let you, this newly baptized infant, hear those words from your Abba:

> "Joe, you are my beloved son;
> with you I am well pleased!"
> "Mary, you are my beloved daughter;
> in you I take great delight!"

Breathe, and let the infant you hear those words from your loving Abba as long as you can bear it.

11

One Freely Done Tithe

How do I learn that my life is not just about me? Nothing works quite like using my wallet/checkbook/onlinebillpay as a prayer book.

Not next year, but on the next payday, send one-tenth, 10%, 1/10 of my next paycheck (10% of gross, not net, if at all possible) to some organization or group of people who are trying to help human beings who live on the margins. If I can't do 10%, then I can't do 10%. What then can I do? If honestly only 1 percent, be grateful for that. The suggestion is **something** from the next paycheck. For spiritual exercise, building a habit as a structure for one's life might be in order.

For best results, the charity ought be one that serves people who are living in poverty, without trying to "fix" their lives, a charity that is a stretch for you (even one you suspect is run by people with an ideology or philosophy different from your own), and anonymous giving is the way to go. For a gift to be *free,* refrain from any instinct to attach strings to control it.

And let it be gone.

12

The Prologue of John

Language problems such as cussin', gossipin' and carryin' on, are mostly a combination of habit and listening when it just ain't right. Respectful and polite disapproval when folks cuss or gossip around us can help others break the habit, but what about when the habitual cuss is me?

I like to go to the Prologue of the Gospel of John. In olden days, John's prologue was called *the little gospel* and read at the end of Sunday Mass. In our day it is the reading for the Mass of Christmas Day, words of a new beginning.

The Greek word ***logos*** could mean *a word spoken* or *a thought that is thought*, understanding God as *speaking* creation into being, or God *thinking* creation into being. We translate it as the word "*Word,*" which we understand as the Son, the second person of the Trinity.

So, the Prologue of John can be a helpful way to remember that I want the words that I use to be the words that God wants people to hear.

John 1:1-17

In the beginning was the Word,
and the Word was with God,
and the Word was God.
He was in the beginning with God.
All things came to be through him,
and without him nothing came to be.
What came to be through him was life,
and this life was
the light of the human race;
the light shines in the darkness,
and the darkness has not overcome it.

A man named John was sent from God.
He came for testimony, to testify to the light,
so that all might believe through him.
He was not the light,
but came to testify to the light.
The true light, which enlightens everyone,
was coming into the world.

He was in the world,
and the world came to be through him,
but the world did not know him.
He came to what was his own,
But his own people did not accept him.

John 1:1-17, continued

But to those who did accept him
he gave power to become children of God,
to those who believe in his name,
who were born
not by natural generation
nor by human choice
nor by a man's decision
but of God.

> And the Word became flesh
> and made his dwelling among us,
> and we saw his glory,
> the glory as of the Father's only Son,
> full of grace and truth.

John testified to him and cried out, saying,
"This was he of whom I said,
  'The one who is coming after me
   ranks ahead of me
   because he existed before me.'"
From his fullness
we have all received,
grace in place of grace,
because while the law was given
through Moses,
grace and truth came
through Jesus Christ.

13

Immensity and Absurdity of Sin

Sin in the world is immense! Suffering can be seen as just part of human life; we will all meet our deaths. And yet there are so many human beings, created in God's own image, who live in de-humanizing suffering like poverty. Most of this can be traced to ignorance and selfishness.

Sin absurd! Why? Because God loves us. How is it not absurd to sin against one who loves us? And yet the human family is the playground of much unnecessary hurting. As it is absurd to wrong a family member who loves us, how could anyone freely sin against this God who loves us beyond measure? It is absurd.

The penance: Simply reflect on the immensity and absurdity of sin.

In his *Spiritual Exercises* (#53), St. Ignatius of Loyola suggests we imagine Jesus on the Cross, be aware of the love that led him to the Cross, and ask: 1. What have I done for Christ?
2. What am I doing for Christ?
3. What do I want to do for Christ?

14

Who Am I That You Care For Me?

God's own workweek of six days creating and one day resting carries a pile of wisdom for us working creatures. Never taking a day of rest will get me sick, and life will spin out of balance.

Part of the Sabbath call is to claim time to give God thanks and praise within a community of believers. Sabbath is also meant to be life-giving, the blessing of time with friends and family, especially with those we do not see all week.

When we see Sabbath work showing up as sin, there might be an unaware suspicion that God is not doing a very good job. So the penance is to be honest with myself: Is there some way I think God could be doing a better job as God? Am I feeling a need to step in and do God's job? Is work on the Sabbath a way of saying I do not trust God? Am I living as if I were God?

See, this is the thing that still blows me away, that God knows *every thing* about me and *still* loves me. Breathe, and pray one of these lines:

Lord, who am I that you care for me? (see Psalm 8:5)
Who am I that you keep me in mind? (see Ps. 144:3)

Pondering the 2nd Week - Exercises 8-14

Ponder in silence whether in Exercises 8 thru 14 something like one of these surfaced:

a seed planted,
something I anticipate taking root and growing within me, and growing me.

a memory provoked,
part of my story, my journey, my identity, aware of gratitude or a desire for healing.

a question raised,
something unknown suggesting research, discussion with others, or more pondering.

an action prompted or resolution made,
a way through which God is calling me.

*Allow at least three minutes for silent pondering,
and then the group may either discuss the ponderings
(restraining the urge to "fix" anybody)
or stay in silence until time is up.*

When time is up: Are there any intercessions from the group?

Our Father ... *and a stanza from the song on page 28?*

Faith of our an-ces-tors, liv\-ing still,
In spite of dun-geon, fire\ and sword;
O how our hearts\ beat high\ with joy
When-'er we hear that glo/-rious Word!

Refrain Faith of our an-ces-tors, ho-ly faith!
We will be true to you till death.

Faith of our fa\-thers, we\ will strive
A-mong all peo-ples, as is our call;
That through the truth\ that comes\ from God,
True free-dom may be found/ by all.

Refrain Faith of our an-ces-tors, ho-ly faith!
We will be true to you till death.

Faith of our mo\-thers, we\ will love
Both friend and foe in all\ our strife;
Liv-ing and preach-ing as love\ knows how
By kind-ly words and vir/-tuous life.

Refrain Faith of our an-ces-tors, ho-ly faith!
We will be true to you till death.

Text: Frederick W. Faber, *Jesus and Mary*, 1849;
refrain by James G. Walton, 1874; altered
Music: ST. CATHERINE, LM with refrain; Henry F. Hemy, 1864;
adapted by James G. Walton, 1874

Exercises 15-21
(3rd Week)
Universal Call to Holiness

SONG (on page 42)

LEADER:

The honor of being a spiritual companion with individual seekers, disciples, ministers, and apostles in the world, is listening in on their lives of prayer.

We are saints and we are sinners. God is calling all of us to sainthood and this does mean being alive in eternity in the love of God in the communion of saints. Indeed it also means letting God form us into the saints that God has created us to be. By the "time" we get to heaven, surely we will have let go of the last of the unforgiven.

Why would it surprise us that God wishes us to live even now as if we were in heaven? That would mean being alive in deep intimacy with God, and accepting the grace to let go of all about us that is unhealed and unforgiven, our unique core wounds. Only in faithful intimacy with God will we be able to accept this grace.

If we have not yet asked for this grace, why not now?

Pause for one minute of silence now and after each exercise.

15

Psalm 65

When a truly hungry person is left with no way to eat except to steal food, the theft is illegal but not necessarily a sin. The rest of us know that stealing is wrong.

Why is stealing wrong? Does this ethic help keep the peace? Is it that we already have enough stuff? Is it the envy that is wrong? Do we steal because life has not given us a fair share?

Psalm 65 is a beautiful creation psalm. One image is rain falling to the earth, loosening the soil so that seeds that have been planted can take root, sprout, and bring forth fruit. God is always sowing seeds into us. Following the parable of the sower, we are called to be good soil, good dirt.

All thanksgiving is rooted in a deep awareness of the intrinsic goodness of reality.
(If these words from a great teacher seem obvious to you, just know they are not to everyone.)

The Penance: Praying through Psalm 65, try to name the raindrops as the many ways that God has blessed you, and follow the psalm with a grateful "thank you" to the Lord.

Psalm 65

To you we owe our hymn of praise,
O God on Zion;
To you our vows must be fulfilled,
you who hear our prayers.
To you all flesh must come
with its burden of wicked deeds.
We are overcome by our sins;
only you can pardon them.
Blessed the one whom you will choose and bring
to dwell in your courts.
May we be filled
with the good things of your house,
your holy temple!

You answer us with awesome deeds of justice,
O God our savior,
The hope of all the ends of the earth
and of those far off across the sea.
You are robed in power,
you set up the mountains by your might.
You still the roaring of the seas,
the roaring of their waves,
the tumult of the peoples.
Distant peoples stand in awe of your marvels;
the places of morning and evening
you make resound with joy.

You visit the earth and water it,
make it abundantly fertile.
God's stream is filled with water;
you supply their grain.
Thus do you prepare it:
you drench its plowed furrows,
and level its ridges.
With showers you keep it soft,
blessing its young sprouts.
You adorn the year with your bounty;
your paths drip with fruitful rain.
The meadows of the wilderness also drip;
the hills are robed with joy.
The pastures are clothed with flocks,
the valleys blanketed with grain;
they cheer and sing for joy.

16

Love is Patient; Love is Kind…

If my rooms were to be buried intact right now by an earthquake, the archaeologists would find the entire room oriented to a box that shows pictures and talks, and they would be reasonable in assuming that the dweller of these rooms had treated that box as a kind of "god."

Infidelity is an old human story. When we are unfaithful, God remains faithful to us. Psalm 117 is the shortest of the psalms, and declares boldly the unfailing fidelity of God, who is always faithful, even when we are not.

Henry Drumond told the story of a man who read St. Paul's "Love is patient, love is kind…" every day for six months, and found it to be a life changing experience. Ponder what might happen were one to read it each day for six months.

The penance is to read 1st Corinthians 13, on three different days. Three days in a row if you remember it, but if you miss a day, just remember on three different days.

1st Corinthians 12:31-13:13

Strive eagerly for the greatest spiritual gifts.
But I shall show you a still more excellent way.

If I speak in human and angelic tongues,
but do not have love,
I am a resounding gong or a clashing cymbal.

And if I have the gift of prophecy
and comprehend all mysteries and all knowledge;
if I have all faith so as to move mountains
but do not have love,
I am nothing.

If I give away everything I own,
and if I hand my body over so that I may boast
but do not have love,
I gain nothing.

Love is patient, love is kind.
It is not jealous,
is not pompous,
it is not inflated,
it is not rude,
it does not seek its own interests,
it is not quick-tempered,
it does not brood over injury,
it does not rejoice over wrongdoing
but rejoices with the truth.

It bears all things,
believes all things,
hopes all things,
endures all things.
Love never fails.

If there are prophecies,
they will be brought to nothing;
if tongues, they will cease;
if knowledge, it will be brought to nothing.
For we know partially
and we prophesy partially,
but when the perfect comes,
the partial will pass away.

When I was a child,
I used to talk as a child,
think as a child,
reason as a child;
when I became a man,
I put aside childish things.

At present we see indistinctly, as in a mirror,
but then face to face.
At present I know partially;
then I shall know fully as I am fully known.

So faith, hope, love remain, these three;
but the greatest of these is love.

17

Lectio Divina at Mass

Lectio Divina means literally *divine* or *sacred reading,* and is most often taught as a way to pray with Scripture, God's revealed word.

Here it can be helpful to remember that it was not until about the year 51 A.D., writing to the Thessalonians from perhaps Athens or Corinth, when Saint Paul wrote the first words written of what we now call the *New Testament.* While the words of liturgy come mostly from Scripture, surely the liturgy was already being celebrated. How appropriate then to use a way of praying with Scripture to pray at Mass, in particular during the readings, the *Liturgy of the Word* !

What's the penance? Next time (at Mass when you remember) listen to the readings for one word or phrase or image that speaks to you.

If your mind wanders during the Mass, breathe, and think to yourself that word or phrase or image. Later, ask the Lord, *why that one?* Consider sharing the word/phrase/image with your family or with a friend.

18

72 Tools of the Spiritual Craft

Catholics like handy lists to help us memorize and remember things we want to know. One of my favorite lists is the so-called *Tools of the Spiritual Craft* from *The Rule* of Saint Benedict. Think of it as a kind of list of the lists.

Take turns reading the 72 with the group. The Penance is to listen for the one thing that may intrigue or grab me as a consolation or as a challenge in my call to live today in God's love.

1. Loving the Lord God with all my heart and soul and strength
2. Loving my neighbors as myself
3. Living by the nonviolence of Jesus
4. Being faithful and committing no adultery
5. Not stealing
6. Not coveting what belongs to others
7. Telling the truth
8. Respecting all people
9. Treating others as I would be treated myself
10. Giving of self in following Christ
11. Taking care of my body as a temple

Tools of the Spiritual Craft, continued

12. Seeking not pleasure first
13. Fasting
14. Befriending the poor
15. Clothing the naked
16. Visiting the sick and those in prison
17. Joining in grief at funerals and wakes
18. Giving aid to those in trouble
19. Comforting the sad
20. Rejecting worldly ways
21. Loving Christ before all else
22. Keeping anger from growing
23. Nursing no grudges
24. Holding no deceit in the heart
25. Making peace without pretense
26. Generosity in charity
27. Avoiding oaths and swearing
28. Speaking the truth with compassion
29. Doing no evil in response to evil done
30. Accepting patiently any injury to self without injuring anyone else
31. Loving our enemies
32. Blessing those who insult us
33. Seeking justice, even at the risk of suffering persecution
34. Growing humble and being not proud

72 Tools of the Spiritual Craft, continued

35. Drinking in moderation, not in excess
36. Eating in moderation, without gluttony
37. Sleeping enough to give the body the rest it needs, but not too much
38. Avoiding lazy sloth
39. Refraining from grumbling or complaining
40. Spreading no slander or gossip
41. Trusting in God alone
42. Giving God the credit for the good one sees in oneself
43. Admitting that the bad things one does are attributable only to oneself
44. Preparing for judgment day
45. Dreading hell and any separation from God who loves me unconditionally
46. Desiring union with God before all else
47. Keeping earthly death before me daily
48. Forming and informing my conscience
49. Knowing that God sees all everywhere
50. Dumping doubts and seeking spiritual counsel
51. Speaking with words God wants to hear
52. Learning to control the tongue
53. Using speech for good and building up
54. Letting joy happen, staying sensitive to those who are unable to laugh

72 Tools of the Spiritual Craft, continued

55. Reading Sacred Scripture and searching for writers who speak God's word to me
56. Praying often, especially with the Psalms
57. Avoiding today my sins of the past
58. Resisting any desires of the flesh that are not consistent with a life of fidelity
59. Loving God's will above my own, knowing that God's will resides at my deepest desire
60. Obeying those who have authority and responsibility for me
61. Desiring to be holy rather than be called holy
62. Fulfilling God's commandments
63. Loving chastity
64. Hating no one, since every human being is made in the image of God
65. Being not jealous or envious
66. Hating strife
67. Making no show of arrogance
68. Honoring and loving the elderly
69. Encouraging and loving the young
70. Praying in the love of Christ for all in enmity
71. Making peace with an adversary before sundown
72. Trusting always in God's mercy

19

Naming My Cross

Remember the story of Jesus being rejected by his own people in Nazareth? (Mark 6:1-6; Matthew 13:54-58; Luke 4:14-30) Jesus calls each disciple to take daily that one's cross and follow him (Luke 9:23).

Saint Ignatius of Loyola invites us to bear in mind that since even the Son of God was rejected by those who thought they knew him, we too ought expect to be rejected. His exercise reminds me of the advice of elder preachers that if no one ever complains about homilies either the preacher is not doing his or her job, or the people are sleeping through them.

Saint Ignatius' exercise goes a bit further by encouraging us to be ready to someday be rejected as Jesus was, even to "savor" a bit the experience of rejection when it happens or when licking our wounds over it.

The Penance is to ponder a question:

Have I yet named my Cross?

20

What's Missing?

In my particular struggles with depression, certain kinds of self-care make all the difference:

1st daily prayer,
2nd sleep,
3rd exercise,
4th healthy food,
5th regular time with family
and friends who know me well,
(and 6th medication which,
  after stubborn attempts to go without,
  I now see as a blessing my ancestors did not have).

They call it *self* care because this is the stuff no one else is going to make us do. You know all this. And you have your own list.

The penance is another question:

> *Lord, what is missing?*

If you know the answer to that question, pray:

> *Lord, help!*

21

My Favorite Gospel Story

Now and again our sinful acting out is rooted in having lost the connection with Jesus that we have felt in the past (or have not known but have always suspected as a possibility).

There can be many reasons for this loss, and there may even be clarity about it. It may have something to do with not being faithful in prayer or in the sacraments or in daily living. If I have no idea why, perhaps God is calling me to a new way of prayer (or calling me back to an old familiar way). So, here's a question:

Is there for me a favorite gospel story
(an event, teaching, or parable)
from Jesus' three-year ministry of
teaching, preaching, and healing?

Not to muddy the water, but just as examples, the parable of the prodigal son and the Easter story of two disciples on the road to Emmaus (both in the gospel of Luke) have each been called "*a* gospel within *the* gospel." Catholics need have no embarrassment over having to ask around for the chapter and the verse.

I ask the question as a penance because of a theory: that there might be for each of us a particular gospel story through which Christ wishes to personally reveal the good news.

If you have a favorite gospel story, then the penance is to read the story again, pretending you've never read it before, and then attempting the Ignatian way of praying a scripture story:

- Read and re-read the story.
- Call on your imagination and be in the story as one of the characters.
- Using all your senses, what do you taste, smell, touch, hear and see?
- Sit for a bit and let the story play out to see what else happens.
- When your time is up, say an *Our Father*; perhaps write a prayer in your journal.
- Consider the possibility of writing out this story in your own hand, keeping it on your person, and reading it every day for, say, a month. (The penance is to *consider* it; whether you *do* it is your free choice).

If you do not yet know your favorite gospel story, consider taking these questions to the Lord?

Lord, do you want a gospel story to be my favorite? How often would you like for me to pray with it?

Pondering Exercises 15-21

Ponder in silence whether in exercises 15 thru 21 something like one of these surfaced:

a seed planted,
> something I anticipate taking root and growing within me, and growing me.

a memory provoked,
> part of my story, my journey, my identity, aware of gratitude or a desire for healing.

a question raised,
> something unknown suggesting research, discussion with others, or more pondering.

an action prompted or resolution made,
> a way God calls me into holiness today.

Allow at least three minutes for silent pondering, and then the group may either discuss the ponderings (restraining the urge to "fix" anybody) or stay in silence until time is up.

When time is up: Are there any intercessions from the group?

Our Father ... *and a stanza from the song on page 42?*

As Ab-ba loves me so do I love you.
I tell you this: re-main in my love.
Keep this com-mand-ment: Love one an-oth-er
As I have loved you, call-ing you friend.

I am the vine and you are my bran-ches;
Let Ab-ba prune you so you bear fruit.
My word re-mem-ber: Love one an-oth-er
As I have loved you, call-ing you friend.

No great-er love than has one to lay down
One's ver-y life for e-ven a friend.
You I have cho-sen: Love one an-oth-er
As I have loved you, call-ing you friend.

You have been with me from the be-gin-ning;
Tes-ti-fy in the Spir-it of truth.
In word and ac-tion: Love one an-oth-er
As I have loved you, call-ing you friend.

Text: from John 15, Stephen J. Wolf, 2007,
tribute to the priesthood of Charley Giacosa
Music: BUNESSAN 5554 D, Scots Gaelic melody
Popular melody for: *Morning Has Broken*

Exercises 22-28
(4th Week)
Vocation "Yes"

SONG (on page 60)

LEADER:

At the turn of the Third Millenium, the Church in North America held a *Congress on Vocations* in Montreal. The genesis of this congress was the prospect of a church with fewer priests. One of the blessings from the gathering was a question:

> *What would it look like*
> *and what difference would it make*
> *if our culture were a "vocation culture"*
> *or a "culture of vocation?"*

The question for the individual is the *vocal* call:

> *What is God calling me to do with my life?*
> *What is God calling me to with today?*

Imagine that our culture and our Church took this question seriously and all of us kept asking this question and we kept helping each other keep asking this question. Would anything be different?

Pause for one minute of silence now and after each exercise.

22

I Have Called You Friends

Be honest. Is not the real reason we judge others a basic fear that there might not be enough of God's love to go around? If I am in competition with everyone else for God's love, then I can find unhealthy solace in the warts, bumps, bruises and lumps of others, especially when I can chortle, *At least I'm not THAT bad!* What a waste of energy.

Judging a person is God's job. None of the rest of us is qualified, because we cannot really know what is going on in the heart of another person. We simply do not have enough data. Daily I wonder if I truly know even what is going on in my own heart. God is the only one who really knows. We can give thanks that the real judge is the one who knows us even better than we know ourselves, our God of mercy!

The penance: breathe a scripture fragment from James, or a gospel canticle from John:

> *There is one lawgiver and judge,*
> *(the One) who is able to save or to destroy.*
> *Who then are you to judge your neighbor?*
> Letter of James 4:12

John 15:9-17

As the Father loves me, so I also love you.
Remain in my love.
If you keep my commandments,
you will remain in my love,
just as I have kept my Father's commandments
and remain in his love.
I have told you this so that my joy may be in you
and your joy may be complete.
This is my commandment:
love one another as I love you.
No one has greater love than this,
to lay down one's life for one's friends.
You are my friends
if you do what I command you.
I no longer call you slaves,
because a slave does not know
what his master is doing.
I have called you friends,
because I have told you
everything I have heard from my Father.
It was not you who chose me,
but I who chose you and appointed you
to go and bear fruit that will remain,
so that whatever you ask the Father in my name
he may give you.
This I command you: love one another.

23

Anger the Jesus Way

This penance is from my answer to Exercise 21, my favorite gospel story. It is the only place where a gospel writer uses the word *anger* or *angry* to describe Jesus. It's not the story of him turning over the tables of the moneychangers; he was probably angry that day, but none of the four gospel writers uses the word there.

In the beginning of the 3rd chapter of Mark, *looking around at them with **anger** and grieved at their hardness of heart*, Jesus speaks to a man with a withered hand.

Jesus gives me a model here for what to do with anger. Remember that anger is a feeling that happens *to* us; the moral question comes in what we *do* with it. So, Jesus experienced the human emotion of anger. What did he do with it?

The Pharisees are watching him and asking themselves whether Jesus will break the law prohibiting work on the Sabbath, by healing the man's withered hand. Jesus knows what they are thinking, and he is the one who can take away all of the fear that pushes them into being judges of others, if they will but engage him in a real conversation. He asks them a riddle, they remain silent, and he is furious. Turning to them with anger, he *grieves* over their hardness of heart, and then does the good thing for the (also silent but obedient) man with the withered hand.

God invites us into the mystery of healing love. When we hide out in the shadows, God invites us with nudge-pokes, desiring to take away all our fear. But God will not violate our freedom. When we choose to stay in what we think is shade safety, does God grieve our being unwilling to risk the gospel riddle, holding this grief in compassion, suffering with us, even when we are unaware of why we are really suffering?

In his humanity, Jesus acknowledges that he is visited with anger. In his divinity, Jesus holds that anger with grief. As both Son of God and son of Mary, he *suffers-with*, he compassions, the Pharisees, who then make plans with their otherwise enemies the Herodians how best to kill him. And Jesus keeps loving them.

The penance: Read the story on the next page, or, revisit *your* favorite.

For more see the author's *Anger-Grief the Jesus Way*, idjc press, 2009.

Mark 3:1-6

Again (Jesus) entered the synagogue.
There was a man there
who had a withered hand.

They watched him closely
to see if he would cure him on the sabbath
so that they might accuse him.

He said to the man with the withered hand,
"Come up here before us."

Then he said to them,
"Is it lawful to do good on the sabbath
  rather than to do evil,
  to save life rather than to destroy it?"
But they remained silent.

Looking around at them with anger
and grieved at their hardness of heart,
he said to the man,
"Stretch out your hand."
He stretched it out and his hand was restored.

The Pharisees went out
and immediately
took counsel with the Herodians against him
to put him to death.

24

Ask To See What God Sees

These may be my favorite words of Jesus:

I have much more to tell you,
but you cannot bear it now.
John 16:12

My response:
Lord, indeed you are correct. I am not ready for it all. But you know my weakness and my strength. You alone know what I am ready for today. So, Lord, that much and only that much, tell me today, what you know I am ready for today (but no more?).

Isn't it something? By all appearances, there are some people with whom I have nothing in common, except that we are both Christians. I know Jews and Muslims with whom I seem to have more in common than some fellow Christians. And yet, it is the person of Jesus who is able to get us each week into the same room and around the same table. Isn't it something?

When I am feeling estranged from a friend or family member, God has graced me with a trinity of ways to take the estrangement to prayer.

1. Imagining that you are sitting with your friend or sibling, put one arm around his or her shoulder, and with the other hand point to him or her and say to our Father, our Abba,
   Abba? Lord? This one is made in your image? I'm having a hard time seeing it. I'm not yet ready to see it all. Abba, but you know how much I can bear. Help me, Abba, to see something of what you see, how this one is made In your image. Abba, thank you.

2. Then, imagining that you are sitting with your friend or sibling, imagine also that Jesus our brother is sitting with you, and pray for yourself and for the other in that most proclaimed gospel passage from Matthew,
   *Our Father,
   who art in heaven, hallowed be your name.
   Your kingdom come, your will be done,
   on earth as it is in heaven.
   Give us this day our daily bread,
   and forgive us our trespasses,
   as we forgive those who trespass against us.
   And lead us not into temptation,
   but deliver us from evil. Amen.*

3. And then, aware that you need the grace that only comes from God, take a deep breath and pray, *Holy Spirit-Breath of God, Help!*

25

Saint Benedict's Twelve Steps to Humility

Pride. Again with the pride. This penance is reserved for students and others who have easy access to a Catholic library or the internet. I ask you to find a little book, *The Rule of Saint Benedict,* written for abbots of monasteries and studied by monks and nuns as part of their formation.

The penance: Find *The Rule,* as it may be called, by Saint Benedict of Nursia, d. 547.

Find Chapter 7 on "Humility" (again with the humility!)

Find in Chapter 7 the **twelve steps** or *stages/levels/etc.* on humility.

Or see the next two pages here.

Pick one of the twelve,;
  memorize it
  (or write it down)
  and take a walk with it.

Saint Benedict's Twelve Steps to Humility
*Previously used by the author in God's Money, idjc press, 2009,
adapted from the 1975 Image Books translation
by Anthony C. Meisel and M.L. del Mastro.*

1st Knowing that God sees me always,
let me live in love with Jesus Christ,
free from fear.

2nd Seeking my deepest, most real desire,
let me follow Christ,
who followed the will of the Father.

3rd Learning that I do not have every answer
and that there are limits to what I can do,
let me seek sources of help and guidance.

4th Admitting that
every worthy commitment in life
involves sacrifice and some difficulty,
let me endure troubles in joyful fidelity.

5th Trusting that God's mercy is endless,
though not my days on earth,
let me honestly confess my sins.

6th Agreeing that all work has dignity,
even the crude and harsh task,
let me be content in my calling.

7th Accepting that for all the gifts and talents
given me by God there will always be
someone more wise, strong and beautiful,
let me see myself as God sees me.

8th Seeing that I do not always have to win
or get my way or be the one who is right,
let me obey the rules of road and life
which have been formed in community.

9th Believing that to judge is the job of God alone,
let me withhold criticism
and unsolicited advice.

10th Having seen misfortune laughed at
and aware of my participation in the hurt,
let me use humor only to give life.

11th Remembering past struggles
to stay awake while others speak,
and the annoying love
of hearing my own voice,
let me use as few words as possible.

12th Grateful to Jesus Christ
who while fully divine
humbled himself as fully human,
even humbling himself on the cross,
let me serve in humble confidence.

26

The Song that Makes Me Say "*YES!*"

A.

Next time at Mass, look around for someone who is having a bad day. Offer your prayers of this Mass for that person, perhaps especially while singing the opening song,

> *For where two or three*
> *are gathered in my name*
> *there am I in the midst of them.*
> Matthew 18:20

B.

What is the song which when we sing at Mass something in you wants to shout, "***Yes!!!***"?

Sing what you know of it. Next time in church look it up in the hymnal and see whether a scripture passage is referenced. If so, that one may be worth visiting.

27

Calendar, Closet, Checkbook and Will

Call to mind your best teacher about life. In your imagination, ask him or her to survey with you your calendar, your closets, your checkbook, and your last will and testament.

Summarize in one sentence what he or she might want to teach you.

_____

_____

_____

_____

28

The At-Hand Stretch

Imagine yourself standing with your arms out, like Leonardo da Vinci's Vitruvian Man, or Jesus on the Cross, and hear these words from our Lord:

> *The Kingdom of God is at hand.*
> Mark 1:15b

Everywhere each of us can reach, touch or go, there is the Kingdom of God, in our midst, especially wherever I can reach or touch or go to another child of God.

Now, stand, hold out your hands as long as you can stand it, and let our Lord say specifically to you by your name:

_____, *the Kingdom of God is at hand.*

Once asked a teen, *Is that weird enough?*
and she smiled, *Yeah, pretty weird.*

Pondering Exercises 22-28

Ponder in silence whether in exercises 22 thru 28 something like one of these surfaced:

a seed planted,
  something I anticipate taking root and growing within me, and growing me.

a memory provoked,
  part of my story, my journey, my identity, aware of gratitude or a desire for healing.

a question raised,
  something unknown suggesting research, discussion with others, or more pondering.

an action prompted or resolution made,
  a way God is calling me to say "Yes!"

Allow at least three minutes for silent pondering, and then the group may either discuss the ponderings (restraining the urge to "fix" anybody) or stay in silence until time is up.

When time is up: Are there any intercessions from the group?

Our Father ... *and a stanza from the song on page 60?*

When/ I sur\-vey the/ won-drous cross
On which the Prince of glo-ry died,
My rich-est/ gain\ I count\ as loss,
And pour con-tempt on all my pride.

For/-bid it\, Lord, that/ I should boast,
Save in the death of Christ my God!
May all vain/ things\ that charm\ me most,
Be sac-ri-ficed as with his blood.

Were/ the whole\ realm of/ na-ture mine,
That trea-sure would be far too small;
Love so a/-ma\-zing, so\ div-ine,
De-mands my soul, my life, my all.

Text: Isaac Watts, *Hymns and Spiritual Songs,* 1707, altered
Music option: ERHALT UNS HERR, LM; Klug's *Geistliche Lieder, 1543;*
Popular melody for: *The Glory Of These Forty Days*
Alternate melody: *Praise God From Whom All Blessings Flow*

Exercises 29-35
(5th Week)
Perfect Act of Love

SONG (see page 76.)

LEADER:

Gandhi has been quoted as having called the free gift of his life by Jesus in the crucifixion the perfect act of nonviolence.

The Christian knows that Jesus freely gave his life out of complete love for all humanity. And so we can paraphrase Gandhi and proclaim Jesus' free gift of his life in the crucifixion as the perfect act of love.

Pause for one minute of silence now and after each exercise.

29

God's Truth, or Psalm 27

The beginning of wisdom is…fear (of) the Lord; she is created with the faithful in the womb.
Wisdom of Ben Sira (Sirach) 1:12

Natural fear is the common sense that avoids unhealthy trouble. Illusory fear keeps our gifts and our true identity hidden under a bushel basket. Fear of the evil one gives too much power to that other guy. Fear of God is the reverential awe worthy of a child of God.

When fear leads to sin, it is fear of or from something other than God. Fear that generates sin is usually rooted in some kind of lie. The antidote is the truth that I believe our God speaks to us each and every moment of each and every day:

I made you; I know you; I love you.

If the source of fear can be named, I might invite you to pray these words, imagining the Lord speaking them to you:

_____, I made you; I know you; I love you.

Or, I might feel moved to ask you to spend some time with the psalm of the unafraid:

Psalm 27

The Lord is my light and my salvation;
whom should I fear?
The Lord is my life's refuge;
of whom should I be afraid?
When evildoers come at me
to devour my flesh,
These my enemies and foes
themselves stumble and fall.
Though an army encamp against me,
my heart does not fear;
Though war be waged against me,
even then do I trust.

One thing I ask of the Lord; this I seek:
To dwell in the Lord's house
all the days of my life,
To gaze on the Lord's beauty,
to visit his temple.
For God will hide me in his shelter
in time of trouble,
He will conceal me in the cover of his tent;
and set me high upon a rock.
Even now my head is held high
above my enemies on every side!
I will offer in his tent
sacrifices with shouts of joy;
I will sing and chant praise to the Lord.

Psalm 27, continued

Hear my voice, Lord, when I call;
have mercy on me and answer me.
"Come," says my heart, "seek his face;"
your face, O Lord, do I seek!
Do not hide your face from me;
do not repel your servant in anger.
You are my salvation; do not cast me off;
do not forsake me, God my savior!
Even if my father and mother forsake me,
the Lord will take me in.

Lord, show me your way;
lead me on a level path
because of my enemies.
Do not abandon me to the desire of my foes;
malicious and lying witnesses
have risen against me.
I believe I shall see the Lord's goodness
in the land of the living.
Wait for the Lord, take courage;
be stouthearted, wait for the Lord!

A NOTE ON PSALM 27

Praying around my fear with this psalm often makes me laugh a bit, because my troubles are really not this bad even when I think they are, though my time may yet come. As the joke goes, though the psalmist might suffer from an undiagnosed paranoia, that does not mean that someone isn't still out to get him!

30

Letter to the Romans, or Romans 8

A parishioner openly shared the most helpful penance he has received, many years ago after confessing a very serious sin: to read the complete letter of Saint Paul to the Romans, especially the wisdom of Chapter 7:

I see the bad and I don't want to do it,
and I do it. Aughghh!
I see the good and I want to do it,
and I don't do it. Aughghh!
Somebody save me from this mess!
paraphrase of Romans 7:15,19

If I sense a desire for a serious penance after a serious sin, and he or she is not playing around, I might suggest the whole Letter of Saint Paul to the Romans, or just the end of Chapter 8:

For I am convinced that neither death, nor life,
nor angels, nor principalities, nor present things,
nor future things, nor powers, nor height, nor depth,
nor any other creature will be able to separate us
from the love of God in Christ Jesus our Lord.
Letter to the Romans 8:38,39

31

The Greatest Command

An old spiritual director promoted a retreat on "The Greatest Sin" and the place was packed.

What is the greatest sin, according to this wise guru? The greatest sin is breaking the greatest commandment. And what is the greatest of the commandments? It is the command of love.

Coach Boots Donnelly told on a radio talk show how the faculty priests were tough disciplinarians when he was a student at Nashville's Father Ryan High School. The cohost asked if such was still the case, and Coach Donnelly said, "Naw… now it's all love, love, love…" I laughed till I cried. A **command** of *love, love, love* almost feels like a contradiction, until we remember that love is the hard work of life.

This penance can be a jolt, and help us see how we sometimes distract ourselves with petty sins to keep from having to take a hard look at our failure to love.

> *This is my commandment:*
> *love one another as I love you.*
> John 15:12

32

Flip Through the Book of Psalms

This penance is to simply flip through the pages of the Book of Psalms, much as one might waste time with a favorite magazine, but with a theoretical question:

> *If I were going to memorize one psalm, which one **would** it be?*

I stress here that the penance is not to actually memorize a psalm, or to find one, or to choose one, but to simply wander through the book with the prayer question.

> *If I were going to memorize one psalm, which one **would** it be?*

33

A Busy Day for Jesus

How often Jesus went off to be alone with his Abba-Father! We might say, "yeah, but that was Jesus; he knew who he was" ("…he was close to his Father…", "…he didn't have a family/boss/reputation to worry about…").

Even Jesus had to figure out how to make time for his Father.

So, the penance is one of those early passages in Mark about Jesus making time for Abba. But before doing the penance, ponder this:

The Son of God felt a human need and a divine desire to take massive doses of solitude alone with our Father. If he both needed and wanted that time, what is it that makes me think I don't need it?

The passage follows the call of the first four disciples and the cure of a demoniac and Simon's mother-in-law:

Mark 1:32-38

When it was evening,
after sunset,
they brought to him all who were ill
or possessed by demons.
The whole town was gathered at the door.
He cured many
who were sick with various diseases,
and he drove out many demons,
not permitting them to speak
because they knew him.

Rising very early before dawn,
he left
and went off to a deserted place,
where he prayed.

Simon and those who were with him
pursued him
and on finding him said,
"Everyone is looking for you."
He told them,
"Let us go on to the nearby villages
that I may preach there also.
For this purpose have I come."

34

To Bed One Hour Early

What time do you usually go to bed? On one election night I stayed up all night watching the returns. The next day, I could not stop eating. My appetite has always been, let's just say, healthy! But this was out of control, and it hit me while pouring more olive oil onto a plate at lunch, "I'm not hungry; I'm tired!" I went to bed an hour early for three nights, saying the Lord's Prayer for someone going to bed truly hungry.

A story is told on television, in the papers, and on those medical talk shows: our sleep patterns are out of whack and our culture is on the whole sleep-deprived.

When I see circles under the eyes and have suggested the penance of going to bed an hour earlier than usual, many gave given sincere thanks.

35

The 2nd Letter of John

Have you read the whole Bible yet? No, the penance is not to read the whole Bible! A penance has to be do-able.

The penance rather is to go to the table of contents of your Bible and write next to the name of each book the *number of chapters* in that book. For the handful of books with only one chapter, write the *number of verses* in that book. Find the shortest book in the Bible (the 2nd Letter of John), read it and the footnotes too, and do your happy dance. (If you do not yet have your own happy dance, then perhaps some creative choreography would be your best penance.)

Then, consider this: One chapter a day of the Bible takes about 44 months, just shy of 4 years, like a high school diploma. Going from the shortest book to the longest is how I finally read the whole Catholic Bible. You know the story already, so bouncing back and forth between Old and New Testaments can be fun. And I promise you *will* find passages that you will know you will revisit, and perhaps dance.

READING THE GOOD BOOK BY THE BOOK

One plan: Begin with the shortest Book (2nd John with 13 Verses) and read through to the longest (Isaiah with 66 chapters). Don't skip the footnotes!

PENTATEUCH
50 Genesis
40 Exodus
27 Leviticus
36 Numbers
34 Deuteronomy

HISTORICAL
24 Joshua
21 Judges
4 Ruth
31 1st Samuel
24 2nd Samuel
22 1st Kings
25 2nd Kings
29 1st Chronicles
36 2nd Chronicles
10 Ezra
13 Nehemiah
14 Tobit
16 Judith
10 Esther
16 1st Maccabees
15 2nd Maccabees

WISDOM BOOKS
42 Job
41 Psalms 1-41
31 Psalms 42-72
17 Psalms 73-89
17 Psalms 90-106
44 Psalms 107-150
31 Proverbs
12 Ecclesiastes
8 Song of Songs
19 Wisdom
51 Sirach

THE PROPHETS
66 Isaiah
52 Jeremiah
5 Lamentations
6 Baruch
48 Ezekiel
14 Daniel
14 Hosea
4 Joel
9 Amos
21vs. Obadiah
4 Jonah
7 Micah
3 Nahum
3 Habakkuk
3 Zephaniah
2 Haggai
14 Zechariah
3 Malachi

THE GOSPELS
28 Matthew
16 Mark
24 Luke
21 John
28 Acts

PAULINE LETTERS
16 Romans
16 1st Corinth.
13 2nd Corinth.
6 Galatians
6 Ephesians
4 Philippians
4 Colossians
5 1st Thess.
3 2nd Thess.
6 1st Timothy
4 2nd Timothy
3 Titus
23vs. Philemon
13 Hebrews

CATHOLIC LETTERS
5 James
5 1st Peter
3 2nd Peter
5 1st John
13vs. 2nd John
15vs. 3rd John
25vs. Jude
22 Revelation

Pondering Exercises 29-35

Ponder in silence whether in exercises 29 thru 35 something like one of these surfaced:

a seed planted,
> something I anticipate taking root and growing within me, and growing me.

a memory provoked,
> part of my story, my journey, my identity, aware of gratitude or a desire for healing.

a question raised,
> something unknown suggesting research, discussion with others, or more pondering.

an action prompted or resolution made,
> a way to pick up my cross daily.

*Allow at least three minutes for silent pondering,
and then the group may either discuss the ponderings
(restraining the urge to "fix" anybody)
or stay in silence until time is up.*

When time is up: Are there any intercessions from the group?

Our Father ... *and a stanza from the song on page 76?*

Ye sons and daugh\-ters of\ the King,
With heav'n-ly hosts\ in glo\-ry sing,
To-day the grave\ has lost\ its sting:
                        Al-le-lu-ia!

On that first morn\-ing of\ the week,
Be-fore the day\ be-gan\ to break,
The Ma-rys went\ their Lord\ to seek:
                        Al-le-lu-ia!

An an-gel bade\ their sor\-row flee,
By speak-ing thus\ un-to\ the three:
"Your Lord is gone\ to Gal\-i-lee":
                        Al-le-lu-ia!

That night th'A-pos\-tles met\ in fear,
A-midst them came\ their Lord\ most dear
And said, "Peace be\ un-to\ you here":
                        Al-le-lu-ia!

Bless-ed are they\ that have\ not seen
And yet whose faith\ has con\-stant been,
In life e-ter\-nal they\ shall reign:
                        Al-le-lu-ia!

And we with ho\-ly Church\ u-nite,
As ev-er-more\ is just\ and right,
In glo-ry to\ the King\ of light: Al-le-lu-ia!

Al-le-lu-ia\! Al-le\-lu-ia! Al-le-lu-ia!

        Text: see John 20; attrib. to Jean Tisserand, d. 1494;
        translated by John M. Neal, 1851, altered
        Music: 888, O FILII ET FILIAE; Chant Mode II,
        Airs sur les hymnes sacrez, odes et noels, 1623

Exercises 36-40
(6th Week)
Wholly New Way

SONG (see page 90)

LEADER:

I sometimes wonder if people in the pews ever tire of hearing my favorite way to describe the Easter mystery:

his wholly new way of being and relating

Pause for one minute of silence now and after each exercise.

36

Four (or Five) toward Intimacy

Entire lifetimes are spent dealing with sins leaking out of our basic human need for intimacy. Here's one parish priest's definition of intimacy:

the grace and gifted capacity to be with another,
who knows you well, accepts you,
and who has direct or implicit permission
to humble you.

Intimacy is when we are able to be with another, as Momma used to say, *without puttin' on airs!* To know and be known is necessary to loving and being loved. Someone who disrespects us enough to choose to be an enemy, or who is still trying to *use* us in some way, or to *fix* us, has not accepted us, and so does not yet see us as God sees us, and so cannot yet love us. Graced intimacy shares the gift of attentive presence free of manipulation.

Friendship is hard work and a gift God wants us to receive. If you seem to have no friends, a.s.k. for them (ask, seek, knock) and keep your eyes open with a willing heart. Ask not only to be loved (God has that covered) but to be a friend.

Henri Nouwen is correct, is he not, in saying that only God can love us the perfect way? To expect any human being to love me perfectly is to expect that person to be God. And so, I will be disappointed. I will then have to forgive.

Every human person has a basic human need for the intimacy of knowing and being known. Intimacy does not have to be genital, but sexual activity that excludes real intimacy is nothing but trouble. Hence the wisdom of marriage.

This need for intimacy is so basic that if we do not tend to it, it will tend to us. When we do not accept the healthy intimacy God intends for us, weirdness happens. For the single person, family and lifelong friends can be the healthiest access to this basic human need.

The penance? Choose one of four:

A. If you are not married, call to mind someone with whom you feel disconnected: a relative, perhaps an old friend who has crossed your mind lately.
Simply ask the question: If you were going to reach out to this person, how would you do so? Meal? Phone call? Letter? Card?
The question is the penance; whether you do anything more than ponder is your call.

B. If you are married, ask God to help you to be creative on the romance front.
Spend some time with the photos and readings from your wedding.
Copy the readings and keep them on your person for a few days of prayer.
Imagine, wherever your spouse is right now, imagine Jesus there too with a hand on his/her shoulder.

C. One old friend describes our sexuality as God's best joke on us.
Imagine your best friend or spouse has caught you in what you know to be an unhealthy activity, and hear him or her say to you in firm love, "Cut that out!"

D. Spiritual masters say that every desire of our heart, even if it is a sinful desire, is some reflection of our deepest longing, which is for God.
Pray with your holy longing, either the first nine verses of Psalm 63 or with parts of Psalm 42.

Again, we tend to this basic human need for intimacy, or it will tend to us.

Psalm 63:2-9

O God, you are my God – it is you I seek!
For you my body yearns; for you my soul thirsts,
In a land parched, lifeless, and without water.

I look to you in the sanctuary
to see your power and glory.
For your love is better than life;
my lips shall ever praise you!

I will bless you as long as I live;
I will lift up my hands, calling on your name.
My soul shall be sated as with choice food,
with joyous lips my mouth shall praise you!

I think of you upon my bed,
I remember you through the watches of the night.
You indeed are my savior,
and in the shadow of your wings I shout for joy.
My soul clings fast to you;
your right hand upholds me.

Psalm 42:2,3,8,12

As the deer longs for streams of water,
so my soul longs for you, O God.
My soul thirsts for God, the living God.
When can I enter and see the face of God?...

Deep calls to deep
in the roar of your torrents,
and all your waves and breakers
sweep over me...

Why are you downcast, my soul,
why do you groan within me?
Wait for God, for I shall again praise him,
my savior and my God.

37

One of the Last Five Psalms

A seminary friend's charismatic prayer group was the chapel-shaped classroom for a way to pray new to me: It is possible to lift up my hands in the air and praise God.

There are those times when the sin being confessed and the way it is described by a penitent suggest a desire give God praise. And there are occasional circumstances which suggest the penitent has already experienced tremendous contrition. When we are in the middle of the mystery of God's mercy we may be most ready to give God praise.

The penance: Give God praise! Go to the end of the Book of Psalms. The last five of the 150 psalms are all psalms of praise. You might follow Jesus' advice on prayer that we hear each year on Ash Wednesday and go to your room, close the door, raise your hands in the air (I only do this with my door closed), and give God praise!

Hallelujah!

38

First Chapter of a Gospel

If it is not a regular habit of prayer, it is good now and then to read one of the four gospel narratives from beginning to end. The penance is to choose one of the four gospels and read the first chapter only, and then consider how a full account of the life, death and resurrection of Jesus Christ might lay over my life story.

Mark is the shortest. John has the smallest vocabulary. Matthew is for the well-off. And Luke is for the poor. Until you get a chance to pick up your Bible, take turns with your group reading an outline of how Charles Dickens organized *The Life of Our Lord* in 1849 writing for his own children. This outline is by one of the great storytellers of the English language.

A question for later:

How might you outline the story?

Outline of THE LIFE OF OUR LORD

Birth of Jesus.
Shepherds of the field and Wise Men of the East.
Murder of the Innocents by Herod the Great.
12-year-old Jesus with the Doctors in the Temple.
Jesus is baptized by John.
Temptation in the Wilderness.
Miracle during the marriage feast at Cana.
Naming of the Twelve.
Great catch of fish.
Teachings on prayer, including the "Our Father."
Healing of a leper, a man with palsy, a servant of a centurion, and a daughter of a magistrate.
Challenges of the Pharisees.
Raising of the only son of the widow of Nain.
Jesus sleeps in the boat in a storm;
Jesus awakes and stills the storm.
Casting of evil spirits into a herd of swine.
Imprisonment and beheading of John the Baptist.
A woman washes Jesus' feet with her hair.
A man ill for 38 years, at the pool of Bethesda.
Feeding of 5,000 plus, from 5 loaves & 2 fish.
Walking on water.
Many more healing miracles.
Feeding of 4,000 plus, from 7 loaves & a few fish.
Sending of the Disciples into towns and villages.
Jesus predicts his Death, Rising, and Ascending.
Transfiguration on Mount Tabor.
Jesus cures a mad boy the Disciples could not.

Outline of THE LIFE OF OUR LORD, continued

Teachings on being childlike
and forgiving 70 times 7 times.
Stories of the unforgiving steward
and a generous master.
Jesus and the accusers of the adulterous woman.
The Greatest Commandment.
Story of the Good Samaritan.
Story of the excuses of those invited to a great supper.
Jesus calls out to Zacchaeus in the tree.
Story of the Prodigal Son.
Story of the Rich Man and Lazarus.
A proud man & a humble man in the Temple.
Jesus is challenged about paying a tax to Caesar.
Example of the widow and her two mites.
Resuscitation of Lazarus of Bethany.
Mary of Bethany anoints Jesus' feet with oil.
Jesus enters Jerusalem on an ass. Hosanna!
Jesus casts out the tables of the money changers.
More of the blind and the lame are healed by him.
Jesus washes the feet of the Disciples.
Jesus says there is one who will betray him.
Judas Iscariot accepts thirty pieces of silver.
The Last Supper.
Jesus predicts that Peter will deny him 3 times.
Jesus prays & the Disciples sleep in Gethsemane.
Judas arrives with a guard and kisses Jesus.
Peter denies Jesus, the cock crows, & Peter weeps.
The Scribes and Priests agree Jesus is to be killed.

Outline of THE LIFE OF OUR LORD, continued

Judas throws the silver at the Chief Priests
and takes his own life.
Chief Priests spend the silver on Potters' Field.
Jesus is questioned by Pontius Pilate.
Pilate has Jesus beaten, mocked, and
crowned with thorns.
Pilate says, "Behold the man!"
Crowds cry, "Crucify him!"
Pilate washes his hands.
Jesus is nailed alive to a great wooden Cross.
Four soldiers divide Jesus' clothes
and gamble over his coat.
People who pass that way mock him.
John the Beloved and four women stay,
including Mary.
A deep and terrible darkness comes over
the whole land.
A soldier puts to Jesus' mouth a sponge
dipped in vinegar.
Jesus says, "It is finished" and
"Father, I commend my spirit."
Joseph and Nicodemus wrap and
bury the body in a new tomb.
Mary Magdalene sees the rolled away stone.
Peter and John the Beloved go into
the empty tomb.
The appearances of the Risen Lord begin.

39

The Breath of the Risen Lord

They wait in the Upper Room, already afraid of persecution, perhaps afraid of Jesus. Most of them had run away from the Cross, and now they hear that he is appearing as the Risen Lord.

He ignores the locked doors, entering with a be-not-afraid, *Peace be with you*. He shows them his wounds, flashes another peace sign, breathes in and onto them, and tells them to *Receive the holy Spirit. Whose sins you forgive are forgiven them, and whose sins you retain are retained.* (John 20:19-23)

God has given to baptized and confirmed followers of Jesus Christ the power to forgive. When we are unable to break free of our human wiring and forgive, we can still breathe in the grace that the Father and the Son are right now Spirit-breathing on and into every Christian.

The forgiveness thing and the love-of-enemy thing and the praying-for-persecutors thing are no doubt the toughest parts of Jesus' teaching. He gives us the grace necessary to say "yes" to this call, and so is right now with the Father breathing in and onto and into you and me. Grace.

40

Claiming Apostleship

They were with him at the Jordan when John baptized him. They were with him in that three-year camping trip of teaching and preaching and healing. Most of them ran away from him on the Cross. They saw him through the Resurrection and the Ascension. And so they now wait for the Spirit to come at Pentecost.

Called by Jesus as *The Twelve* but now eleven, they go about choosing a successor to Judas. In their midst, Peter speaks, "Therefore, it is necessary that one of those who accompanied us the whole time the Lord Jesus *came and went among us, beginning from the baptism of John until the day on which he was taken up from us,* become with us *a witness to his resurrection.* (Acts 1:21-22)

Just as the Old Testament is part of who Jesus is, you know the story of Jesus because it is part of your story, which is how we tell it.

The penance is one more question:

How might I tell the great story
of the Baptism, Ministry, Death and Resurrection
to a neighbor who wants to understand who I am?

Pondering Exercises 36-40

Ponder in silence whether in exercises 36 thru 40 something like one of these surfaced:

a seed planted,
something I anticipate taking root and growing within me, and growing me.

a memory provoked,
part of my story, my journey, my identity, aware of gratitude or a desire for healing.

a question raised,
something unknown suggesting research, discussion with others, or more pondering.

an action prompted or resolution made,
a way God is calling me to be fully alive.

*Allow at least three minutes for silent pondering,
and then the group may either discuss the ponderings
(restraining the urge to "fix" anybody)
or stay in silence until time is up.*

When time is up: Are there any intercessions from the group?

Our Father ... *and a stanza from the song on page 90?*

GOING TO CONFESSION

I avoided the sacrament of reconciliation for years because I had forgotten how to go. Please don't. The most difficult part is showing up. We go to confession in our hearts every Sunday at the beginning of Mass, and say together, *Lord, have mercy; Christ, have mercy; Lord, have mercy*. And then the priest prays an actual prayer of absolution for those everyday sins.

If you have forgotten how to go, or how to say an act of contrition, either look it up on the internet or, better yet, just go and ask the priest for help with the process. If the priest is perturbed by this, give sympathy for his bad day, thank him for trying, and go find another one.

The sacrament of reconciliation is in a sense the big gun for those major things that we keep dragging around like a ball-and-chain. In my own life of faith, when there are one or two or three things still dragging down my freedom, it's time again for the sacrament of dynamite. Again, the hard part is showing up.

And again, many Catholics do not seem to know that it is the priest's job to propose a penance, and then the penitent, the one confessing the sins, is on for either accepting the penance or asking for another one. We might not be ready yet to send a greeting card to an estranged relative or reach out to a neighbor, and that's a fair thing to bring up.

My Favorite EXAMINATION OF CONSCIENCE
from World Youth Day 2002

Following the example of the prodigal son (Luke 15) reflect on your life with neither condemnation nor complacency, and allow the Holy Spirit to show when you have acted contrary to the teaching of our Lord Jesus Christ in thought, word or deed.

IN RELATION TO GOD

- Am I offering myself for spiritual growth? How? When?
- Is my heart set on God, so that I really love God above all things?
- Are private prayer and Sunday worship a priority?
- Have I love and reverence for the name of God?
- Am I hesitant or ashamed to give witness in my life to my faith in God?
- Do I turn to God only when I am in need?
- How am I responding to my baptismal commitments to witness to Christ and to be a person of faith, hope and love?

IN RELATION TO OTHERS

- Are there any relationships that are giving me concern today?
- Am I quick to forgive and slow to judge?
- Do I use others as a means to an end?
- Do I take care of people who are poor or sick or defenseless?
- Am I sincere and honest in my dealings with others?
- Have I been the cause of another person committing sin?
- Do I care for and respect the environment in which I live?

IN RELATION TO MYSELF

- Do I truly believe that I am made in the image and likeness of God and therefore am one of God's wondrous creations?
- Am I too concerned about myself, my health, and my success?
- Do I really live as a Christian and give a good example to others?
- What do I spend most of my time thinking about?
- Have I kept my senses and my whole body pure and chaste as a temple of the Holy Spirit?
- Do I bear grudges; do I contemplate revenge?
- Do I seek to be humble and an instrument of peace?

A CELEBRATION OF RECONCILIATION

A. Exchange greetings with the priest.
Then together make the sign of the cross:
> ✛ *In the name of the Father, and of the Son,*
> *and of the Holy Spirit. Amen.*

B. If you want, ask the priest to say a prayer for you, or to help you.

C. You then confess your sins.
The priest may help you by asking questions and offering encouragement and advice.

D. The priest will propose an act of penance - an act of amendment of life and satisfaction of sin.

E. You will be invited to express sorrow for sin (or to make an act of contrition).
You may recite the *Act of Contrition*, compose your own prayer of sorrow, or use these or similar words:
> *Father, I have sinned against you*
> *and am not worthy to be called your son/daughter.*
> *Lord Jesus Christ, Son of the Living God,*
> *have mercy on me, a sinner.*

F. The priest offers a prayer of absolution using the ritual prayer of the Church. You respond: *Amen.*

G. The priest may invite you to praise God, saying:
> *Give thanks to the Lord, for he is good.*

You may respond:
> *God's mercy endures for ever.*

H. The priest may send you forth, saying:
> *The Lord has freed you from your sins.*
> *Go in peace.*

You may respond:
> *Thanks be to God.*

ACKNOWLEDGMENTS

I make no claim to having invented any of these penances; these are the sources I remember. If there is theological trouble with any of them, the fault is my own. If an attribution is omitted, please let me know so I can make it right.

Sin, Introduction, page 8. One of the precepts of the Church is to confess sins at least once a year, which becomes essential in cases of serious sin (Catechism paragraphs 2041-43). *For a sin to be mortal* (also called serious or grave), *three conditions must together be met:*

> *Mortal sin is sin whose object is **grave matter** and which is also committed with **full knowledge** and **deliberate consent**.* (Catechism paragraph 1857)

Love Letter from God, page 11: from *31 Days of God's Love-Call,* meditation rendering of scripture from the first week of the *Spiritual Exercises of Saint Ignatius of Loyola,* Stephen Joseph Wolf, idjc press, 2013.

#1 page 12, *Sit with it without thinking about it.* Thomas Keating, OCSO, & Tom S., *Divine Therapy & Addiction,* Lantern Books, 2009, page 39.

#3 page 15, *A tree gives glory to God by being a tree.* Thomas Merton, Trappist monk, *New Seeds of Contemplation,* New Direction Books, 1961, page 29.

#4 page 17, *Balance Sheet.* Franciscan friar of the 15th century Luca Pacioli is called by many the father of double-entry accounting.

#6 page 21, *Humility is reality; pride is illusion.* From Fr. Vincent Tobin, OSB, on a retreat at Saint Meinrad Abbey in Indiana.

#7 page 26, *God's Ones.* The 1 1 1 1 1 census of God is from a class of Fr. Larry Hennessey at Mundelein Seminary north of Chicago. Once doing this in a classroom of children, I missed one little boy, and he ran up front and said, "Do me too!" Thanks, Larry.

#9 page 32, *Un-telling a Lie.* From Pat Bradley, while working together at the Downtown Nashville YMCA.

#11 page 35, *One Freely Done Tithe.* For more, see *God's Money* by the author, idjc press, 2009, and *Money and Freedom, the New American Game* by the author when a CPA and Eric B. Dahlhauser, CPA, 1992.

#13 page 39, *Spiritual Exercises of Saint Ignatius of Loyola.* This is a very small taste of the exercises. The best way to experience them for the first time is on a 3-day, 5-day or 8-day retreat at a Jesuit retreat house.

#14 page 40, *Work on the Sabbath as a sign of lack of trust in God.* I thought this notion was from Harold S. Kushner's *To Life,* or from Abraham Joshua Heschel's *I Asked for Wonder,* but could not find it in either.

Core wound, page 43. Studying spiritual direction through the *Institute for Priestly Formation* based at Creighton University, the articulation of the unique core woundedness of each human has been very helpful in my Christian journey. Thanks, IPF.

#15 page 44, *When a truly hungry person is left with no way to eat except to steal food*... This example from moral theology flows from our understanding that all of creation is a gift to all of humanity, with an abundance meant by God to meet the needs of all.

#15 page 44, *All Thanksgiving*... This phrase might have been a throwaway comment by Fr. Larry Hennessey, but it hit something deep inside me.

#16 page 47, *Love is Patient; Love is Kind*... Henry Drummond's story is in his booklet *The Greatest Thing in the World*, 1889.

#18 page 51, *72 Tools of the Spiritual Craft*. Saint Benedict of Nursia, d. 547, *The Rule*, chapter 4. The Liturgical Press 1982 translation edited by Timothy Fry, O.S.B. calls them *The Tools for Good Works*. Neither title ought minimize the necessity of grace.

Vocation Culture, page 61. *Conversion, Discernment, Mission: Fostering a Vocation Culture in North America*, Report on the 2002 North American Congress on Vocations in Montreal, USCCB, 2003.

#22 page 62, *Competition for God's Love*. Mundelein Seminary teacher Fr. Robert Barron honed in on this message with right regularity. Thanks, Bob.

#23 page 64, *Anger the Jesus Way*. This is a three-page summary of *Anger-Grief the Jesus Way* by the author, idjc press, 2009.

#25 page 69, *Twelve Steps to Humility*. Saint Benedict of Nursia, d. 547, *The Rule*, chapter 7, on Humility.

#31 page 82, *The Greatest Sin*. This spiritual director so full of wisdom was Fr. Vince Malatesta, S.J.

#36 page 93, *Only God can love us perfectly*. Henri Nouwen, *Bread for the Journey*, Harper San Francisco, 1997, entry for January 20.

#38 pg. 99, *The Life of Our Lord*. Charles Dickens, 1849.

#40 page 103, *Claiming Apostleship*. Study everything about charisms you can get your hands on from the *Catherine of Siena Institute*. I am so grateful to Sherry Weddell for her ministry. Please do visit siena.org.

Scripture

Psalm 8:5	40	Mark 1:15b	74
Psalm 23	31	Mark 1:32-38	85
Psalm 27	79	Mark 3:1-6	66
Psalm 42:2,3,8,12	96	John 1:1-17	37
Psalm 46	13	John 15:9-17	63
Psalm 63:2-9	95	John 15:12	82
Psalm 65	45	John 16:12	67
Psalm 104	22	John 20:19-23	102
Psalm 131	14	Acts 1:21-22	103
Psalm 144:3	40	Romans 8:38,39	81
Isaiah 43:1-5a	19	1st Corinth. 13	48
Sirach 1:14	78	James 4:12	62

CPSIA information can be obtained at www.ICGtesting.com
Printed in the USA
LVOW12s2003090214

372953LV00001B/2/P